CLASSIC POPULAR

SOLOS, DUETS & TRIOS FOR Clarinet

Arranged by JOHN CACAVAS

CONTENTS

LOVE IS HERE TO STAY

Music and Lyrics by
GEORGE GERSHWIN and IRA GERSHWIN

I GOT RHYTHM

Music and Lyrics by
GEORGE GERSHWIN and IRA GERSHWIN

IF9659

THE MAN I LOVE

Music and Lyrics by
GEORGE GERSHWIN and IRA GERSHWIN

IF9659

THEME FROM "ICE CASTLES"
(Through the Eyes of Love)

Lyrics by
CAROLE BAYER SAGER

Music by
MARVIN HAMLISCH

Slowly with feeling

FORTY-SECOND STREET

Lyrics by
AL DUBIN

Music by
HARRY WARREN

IF9659

SONG FROM "M*A*S*H"
(Suicide is Painless)

Words and Music by
MIKE ALTMAN and JOHNNY MANDEL

DAYS OF WINE AND ROSES

Lyrics by
JOHNNY MERCER

Music by
HENRY MANCINI

CAN YOU READ MY MIND?
(Love Theme from "Superman")

Words by
LESLIE BRICUSSE

Music by
JOHN WILLIAMS

TEACH ME TONIGHT

Words by
SAMMY CAHN

Music by
GENE DePAUL

I COVER THE WATERFORNT

Words by
JOHN GREEN

Music by
EDWARD HEYMAN

THE WIND BENEATH MY WINGS

Words and Music by
LARRY HENLEY and JEFF SILBAR

20
24
3
mf
29
34

Theme from

THE MAGNIFICENT SEVEN

by ELMER BERNSTEIN

IF9659

THE SUMMER KNOWS
(Theme from "THE SUMMER OF '42")

Words by
MARILYN and ALAN BERGMAN

Music by
MICHEL LEGRAND

IF9659

JEEPERS CREEPERS

Words by
JOHNNY MERCER

Music by
HENRY WARREN

Nominee, Best Song, 1957

TAMMY

Words and Music by
JAY LIVINGSTON and RAY EVANS

LOVE AND MARRIAGE

Lyrics by
SANMMY CAHN

Music by
JAMES VAN HEUSEN

STAR WARS
(Main Theme)

Music by
JOHN WILLIAMS

IF9659

THE VARSITY DRAG

Words and Music by
B. G. DeSYLVA, LEW BROWN
and RAY HENDERSON

IF9659

FIDDLER ON THE ROOF
(Prologue)

Lyrics by
SHELDON HARNICK

Music by
JERRY BOCK

AS TIME GOES BY

Words and Music by
HERMAN HUPFELD

SUMMERTIME

Words and Music by GEORGE GERSHWIN
DuBOSE and DOROTHY HEYWARD
and IRA GERSHWIN

IF9659

DANCING IN THE DARK

Words by
HOWARD DIETZ

Music by
ARTHUR SCHWARTZ